100 Exciting Reasons To Write A Book!

Also by Earma Brown

Write Your Best Book Now! (paperback)
How to Write a Book In 100 Days (paperback)
eBook it! (ebook)
Article Marketing Speedway (ebook)
Self Publishing Your Way Now (ebook)
40+ Article Writing Templates (ebook)

Visit http://butterflypress.net/store/

100 EXCITING REASONS
TO WRITE A BOOK!

During Good Times & Tough Times

Earma Brown

Butterfly Press
Dallas, Texas

EPIGRAPH

Books are the treasured wealth of the world and the fit
inheritance of generations and nations.

—Henry David Thoreau

TABLE OF CONTENTS

100 EXCITING REASONS TO WRITE A BOOK

INTRODUCTION

Dear Aspiring Author:

Have you wondered why you should write your very own book this year? This is the book for you! I designed this book to offer you 100 exciting reasons that you should put pen to paper and keep going to completion.

You'll come away pumped and ready to GET IT DONE. You'll know you should get started and complete for reasons like:

- now is better than later.

- create another income stream.

- make your mother proud.

- expand your client base.

- zoom past your competitors without a book and more...

I've included popular sections from my 100 DAYS TO A BOOK COURSE like *How To Give Your Book The Test Of Significance* to see if it will sell before you write it. And the *21 Writing Mistakes That May Stamp S.T.A.L.E. On Your Book* including how to correct them and write compelling copy.

My hope is that you read it and be inspired; then consider it a perfect gift for any aspiring author you know. Or get one for every writer in your writers group. Remember, if you enjoy the journey life is made easier.

To your writing success,

Earma Brown

CHAPTER 1

10 OVERALL GOOD REASONS
TO WRITE A BOOK

We all have to start with ourselves. It is time to walk the talk.
Take the journey of making very difficult decisions. Start
removing things from your life that are not filling your cup
and adding things that bring joy in to your life.

—*Lisa Hammond, Author of Dream Big*

*H*ave you developed your career, business or service in excellence? If so, it deserves the greatest opportunity for growth you can afford it right?

A great way to get more leads, more sales and more customers is to use one of the fastest growing tools around to help you connect with more prospects. A book will expand your exposure and increase your sales opportunities.

Here are 10 good reasons to write a book:

1. Add an additional income stream. You may have already built a respected name for yourself in your career or business. A book will bring you even more respect. The growing group of people who gleam insight from you will love your information is finally in book form. They will reward you by buying from you. They will love the convenience and concrete gratification of reading your information in a book.

2. Expand your reach to the world. When your book is made available, many people will purchase from all over the world. It will open the opportunity for you to interact with people outside of your immediate area. When your subscribers and customers have good success with your book they will tell their friends and associates. Referrals make the best customers for they bring a higher rate of sales.

3. Build your brand name and enhance your prestige as a professional. Let your readers know why your book is the best choice. Build quality into your work so your customers will enjoy spreading the word about your book. As I am sure you have heard before, your customers are your best marketers.

4. Create a greater awareness of your business by offering free articles and tips to your book readers and website visitors. People are always looking for good information, a whopping 85% of Internet users are looking for information.

Make your intent to give something useful and helpful in your area of expertise. As your visitors come for the free, they will become aware of your book and services. They may not buy the first or even the fifth time but expert statistics say up to 50% will buy.

5. Create a powerful business card. Offer your book audience original, different information. Have you wondered what makes a new diet book sell well even when there are scores of diet books on the market?

The author presents their unique set of successful diet rules, their exercise program, their perspective, their testimonials and their credentials. They use original, different information for the same results.

6. Inspire a life full of adventure and opportunities. Inspire people to do something good. Weave inspiring stories into your book and sell more. The 21 Irrefutable Laws of Leadership spent 18 straight months on the Business Week Business Best Seller List. Dr. Maxwell started each chapter with a short story of a famous person successfully using the chapter's law of leadership.

7. Entertain your audience with drama, humor or fun. Enrich the lives of your customers. Do you have a talent to make people laugh? Use it in your book. Provide a little oasis of escape for your readers. People love it when you entertain them.

Intertwine funny stories into your non-fiction manuscript. Entertain them, make them laugh; they'll love you for it. Best of all, they will have fun telling all their friends about your funny book.

8. Give a greater understanding of life. Have you been gifted with a deep understanding of life? Put small excerpts of your understanding throughout your book. Sprinkle your quotes along with other famous philosophers or world thinkers within your book.

9. Elevate your name to fame. Write a book filled with success experiences that motivate your audience to do more, give more or share more. Share your experiences to motivate your audience. Share how you overcame seemingly insurmountable challenges in your field. It will motivate your audience to think if you did it; they can do it too.

10. Offer solutions to your audience. Offer the magic pill or simple steps to solve a problem in your field. Every one loves it when we get simple solutions to our problems. Get this right and you could have a best seller. Do you know the solution to a vexing problem? Write the solution in your book. You might be surprised at who's searching for a little relief.

You have grown your career, business or service; now write a book to enjoy watching your profits soar to new heights. Then remember stay in touch with your buyers. When they order a book from you follow up with them. Start building your list and send them regular follow-up information, free bonuses and requests.

CHAPTER 2

10 STRATEGIC REASONS TO WRITE A BOOK

However beautiful the strategy, you should
occasionally look at the results.

—Winston Churchill

Are you ready to take your career to the next level? If you are a speaker, seminar leader, consultant, coach, writer, service business owner or an expert in your field you might be interested in writing a book.

Put your insightful message in book form and watch it catapult your career to the next level. Interested? Here are ten more good reasons you should write a book:

1. A book captures your unique insightful information. You have specific skills and information. Thousands of people search for specific information daily. They want simple to read and easy to understand information.

Write a book to educate your audience; include engagement tools in your book. Help them make more money, cut costs or solve their problems. Examples include: online assessments, how to tips, short reports, resource lists, how-to tutorials, dictionary of terms in your field and more.

2. A book builds extra credibility to your message. People are more likely to value your message in book form. People want to listen to what you have to say. It carries status that's not quite captured in other formats like tapes, cds or even video.

3. A book crystallizes your message. Write a book and it will focus your personal or even professional mission. People will take notice because author stands behind your name. Your book expresses your message in a clear permanent format.

4. A book expands your audience. Speakers reach 100s through the speaker's circuit on a regular basis. A book will potentially reach 1000s. It takes on a life of its own. Even in the 21st century a book may travel and capture an audience that even televised media can't go.

5. A book distinguishes you in a crowd. Your professional associates may be used to competing and winning more business. Write a book and leverage higher fees for the same amount of work. Leave your pro associates in the dust with author behind your name.

6. A book brings a new level of fame. Write a book to elevate your name in your field. More people will know about you and gain respect for your expert knowledge through a book.

7. A book creates greater opportunities for profit. Write your book and create other products that complement or follow up your original work. You can create cds, courses or podcasts from the material in your book.

8. A book is your new networking card. Write a book to provide your potential reader with new, special information. Have you thought about what makes a new fitness book sell well even when there are scores of weight loss and fitness books on the market?

The author presents their exclusive set of successful rules, their program, their viewpoint, their case studies and their credentials. They use unique, similar but different information for the same results. Make your book your best networking card yet.

9. A book creates a world of opportunities. Offer your readers an opportunity to learn something new or interesting. Sprinkle your book with little known interesting facts about your topic.

Be careful to avoid information overload with pages of detailed statistics. But if you sprinkle them as morsels throughout your book, you create anticipation that will lead your readers through to the end. People love statistics and bite-sized trivia about just about any topic.

10. A book makes it simple. Give your readers an easy to read style to learn about something. Take a complex subject in your field and make it simple. Most people enjoy an easy reading language.

They will not only reward you by reading to the end but your readers will be happy to tell all their friends about your insightful easy to read book.

Don't put it off any longer. Focus in on your good reasons to write a book. Your audience needs your insightful advice. Just do it and watch your career take off to new levels.

CHAPTER 3

7 EXCITING REASONS TO WRITE A BOOK

Think BIG. There are unseen forces ready to support your dreams.

—Cheryl Richardson, Author

Have you been dreaming of writing a book this year? According to a recent survey the New York Times reported, 81% of people feel that they have a book in them and should write it. Why not join the list of authors who acted on that thought?

Writing a book is a great way to position you to go global with your message, create additional income streams and go on more vacations. A book will expand your exposure, add credibility and increase your opportunities for adventure.

Still not convinced? Here are 7 more exciting reasons you should write a book now:

1. Write a book now; for now is better than later. Kill procrastination by acting now. Sign up for a course? Read a good book about book writing. Sketch out your book writing plan. Remember you become a successful author the minute you start moving toward your worthwhile book goal. I don't know anyone that regrets they wrote a book. But I know plenty of people that regret they didn't do it sooner.

2. Write a book and create a referral machine. When your book is published and ready to sell, people will visit your website and buy it from all over the world. With your book going around the world, opportunities for you to interact with people outside of your local area will come.

Therefore, write a good book and make it easy for your customers to tell their friends. Put a tell-a-friend form on your book's website to encourage the magic of referrals. Offer a free gift related to your book to urge even more referrals.

3. Write a book and go places you've never gone. At the least, your book will travel to countries and places you've never gone. Better yet, add speaking about your book's topic to your list of services and watch new doors and opportunities for you open. Either way, writing your book will open opportunities to go places you may not get to go any other way.

4. Write a book and create multiple income streams. Don't just plan a one book event but plan a series of books. It's important to expand your thinking to the possibilities after your book is published.

Plan to produce articles, books and updates that help your readers and help you profit from your passion. Each new book or related material will create new profit opportunities, further enhance your visibility and reinforce your credibility as an expert.

5. Write a book and become famous. Grow your name to fame. Write a book filled with success experiences that motivate your audience to give more, do more or share more. Share your experiences to inspire your audience.

Share how you overcame seemingly insurmountable challenges in your field. It will motivate your audience to think if you did it; they can do it too.

6. Write a book and make your mother proud. Intertwine stories into your non-fiction manuscript. Entertain your audience, make them laugh; they'll love you for it. Best of all, your family, your friends and your mother will be so proud to tell all their friends about your book.

7. Write a book and get paid higher fees. Writing a book elevates you to expert level. You gain instant credibility just by having author behind your name? And that added credibility gives you the power to increase your fees to expert level up to 400% and more.

Are you ready to join the ranks of successful authors? You don't have to call your family to tell them you'll be late again today.

You won't even have to pull in more people to help you work harder. I can't think of a more opportune way to change your bottom line and even your life than by writing a book. Go ahead; write your best book now and prosper.

CHAPTER 4

7 PROFITABLE REASONS
TO WRITE A BOOK

*You have a clean slate every day you wake up. You have a chance
every single morning to make that change and be the person you
want to be. You just have to decide to do it. Decide today's the day.
Say it; this is going to be my day.*

—*Brendon Burchard Author of The Millionaire Messenger*

❧

*A*re you ready to add a new profit stream to your life? Write a book
this year and discover new ways to get extra money. What could you
do with extra money? I have a few ideas. With new income streams, you
could fund your dream vacation. You could help pay the bills with money
left over. You could elevate your lifestyle.

Or better yet, write a book and launch a whole new career. Now
that you've thought about what to do with your extra money, here are 7
profitable reasons to write a book to grow your business:

1. Write a book and gain credibility. When you write your own book,
people will more readily trust you. Remember, whether you are selling
products or services people tend to buy more and do business with people
they trust. We love doing business with our trusted friends.

A book sets you apart from the non-author colleagues in your field.
Write a book this year and receive a boost of profits from your clients
because they trust you.

2. Write a book and become global. After releasing your book to the
world, you become global. You have the ability to reach out and touch

someone across the globe. Your customers may live in your neighborhood or across the world in another country. A book will extend your reach and profits to new areas.

3. Write a book and start a new career. You can use your new book to launch a new career. Or you can simply use a book to leverage your existing career to new levels. With your book, you can consider starting a career in publishing, speaking or consulting in your field.

4. Write a book and create an ebook. Develop your book into an ebook. Technology has advanced making it easier and easier to electronically publish your own e-books. The profits from each sale on a per-unit basis can be 10X the royalties earned by your original book. For example, at the time of this writing Amazon announced that for every 100 paperbacks sold, it sells 115 Kindle e-books.

5. Write a book and become the expert. Become the go to guy or gal in your field. Pull potential book readers in with free articles and tips to help them. People are always looking for good information, a whopping 85% of Internet users are looking for information. Supply them with good information and they will think of you (a trusted expert) when they're ready to buy.

6. Write a book and grow a database of potential clients. Put a sign-up form on your book's website. Give away something free to entice your visitors to sign-up. Develop newsletters, columns, courses based on the information gathered for your book.

Email newsletters offer you another opportunity to keep in touch with your readers. Your newsletters can be either informational or opinionated. Either way, they give you an opportunity to remain visible, grow your list and build even more credibility.

7. Write a book and create other products from it. Write your book in chunks, chapters, sections and parts. Writing this way will allow you to refine, repeat and repackage your information. Develop a continuing with a website and a stream of follow-up products and even services to build your book, your brand and your profits further.

If you don't get started writing your book this year, you may never receive the additional profits you deserve. So go ahead; write a book and start growing your extra profits today.

CHAPTER 5

7 EXCITING THINGS TO DO AFTER YOU WRITE A BOOK

Patience and perseverance have a magical effect before which difficulties disappear and obstacles vanish.

—John Quincy Adams, Sixth U.S. President

Are you tired of waiting for something exciting to happen in your life? Don't wait any longer; take destiny in your own hands. Join the list of authors who finally created some excitement in their life by writing their very own book?

Would it excite you to receive a growing monthly income from a book you wrote? How exciting would it be to fund a much needed vacation with the additional income stream your book created for you?

Most people are excited when their appointment book is filled with cream of the crop clients that don't mind paying top dollar for their services as an expert author. Still not convinced you get to do exciting things when you write your book?

Here are 7 more exciting things you get to do after you write your book:

1. Rise above the rest. If you've been looking for a way to rise above your competition, writing a book will elevate you above your competitors without a book. Do a good job with your book, promote it and it may catapult you into stardom.

2. Put your book in the local library. After you write your book you become one of your city's local authors. Before you finish apply for a LCCN number. The Library of Congress Control Number or LCCN is a serially based system of numbering cataloguing records in the Library of Congress in the United States.

3. Change people's perspective of you. Are you dissatisfied with the way people treat you. Does someone always perceive your opinion as less than your friend or work associate? A client of mine said, "My colleagues didn't take my views serious until my book came out. Now, I'm constantly asked what I think about the problems that come up."

4. Choose only the cream of the crop clients. Your cream of the crop clients respect you as an expert author and come to you for solutions. They value your expertise and don't mind paying to benefit from your knowledge.

5. Create a prescription. No I don't mean a medical prescription. We'll leave that to the medical doctors. What I mean is offer a system or set of steps that will result in a solution. Every one loves it when we get simple solutions to our problems. Get this right and you could have a top seller.

Do you know the solution to a pressing problem? Write the solution in your book. You might be surprised at the relief you can offer inside your book. Your readers will be grateful and become your best referrals telling everyone about your book.

6. Travel the world. Does travel excite you? For some, it excites them to go to new cities or to a country they've never been before. Well, pack your bags! Writing your book opens the door of opportunity to go places you've never been before.

Add speaking about your book's topic to your list of services and watch even more new doors and opportunities for you open.

7. Produce a 24 hour salesman. Write your book and watch it become your hardest working salesman. It doesn't require any time off or sick leave. If promoted properly and set up on the Internet, it just keeps going and going like the Energizer bunny.

Are you excited about the possibilities waiting for you on the other side of completing your book yet? Don't keep waiting for excitement to happen to you. You could be this time next year looking for that experience.

Go ahead; write your very own book. Then jump around and get excited about the wonderful things you get to do. Here's to seeing your name in print!

CHAPTER 6

7 PROFITABLE THINGS TO DO
AFTER YOU WRITE A BOOK

The individual who wants to reach the top in business must appreciate the might of the force of habit and must understand that practices are what create habits. He must be quick to break those habits that can break him and hasten to adopt those practices that will become the habits that help him achieve the success he desires.

—*J. Paul Getty, 1892-1976, American Oil Tycoon*

❧

Are you tired of waiting for your bottom line to change? Don't wait any longer; take your profit line into your own hands. Join the list of authors who finally wrote their book and profited from doing so?

Would you like to receive monthly passive income from a book you wrote? What would you do with the extra cash each month? You might consider a vacation in Hawaii or the Bahamas. Some friends of mine just got back from Jamaica.

After your book is written and published you can enjoy seeing your appointment book fill up with clients excited to do business with you. They like you and trust you because they just read your book. Still not convinced you get to do profitable things when you write your book? Here are some ways to gain profitable leverage when you write your book:

1. **Write your book and grow your assets.** Robert Kiyosaki author of Rich Dad Poor Dad says, "In simple terms, anything that puts money, or income, into your pocket is classified as a financial asset." When you write a top selling book that puts money in your pocket

every month, you can list your book as an asset on your financial statements.

2. **Write your book and get interviewed on a local radio show.** As an author of a book, you become the *go to guy or gal* in your field. On the show, people call in and ask you questions about your expertise. Because you wrote a book, they trust your advice.

3. **Write your book and sign up for a booth or table.** As a celebrated author, you get to sign up for a table at a street fair and sell your book. You will meet people who just want to talk about your subject

4. **Write your book and create an electronic product.** Develop your book into an ecourse or an email workshop. Technology has advanced making it easier and easier to electronically create your book into an information product. The profits from each sale on a per-unit basis can be 10X the royalties earned by your original book.

5. **Write your book and develop an information empire.** Now that you've finished your book, don't stop there; take it a few steps further. You can create other products from it. Just divide it into chunks, sections and parts developing booklets, courses, cds and more.

   Dividing your book this way will allow you to refine, repeat and repackage your information. You can keep developing your book with a website and a stream of follow-up products and even services to build your brand and your profits further.

6. **Write your book and offer a new services in your business.** You can use your new book to launch a new service in your business. Or you can simply use a book to leverage your existing services to new levels. With your book, you can consider starting a career in publishing, speaking, teaching, coaching or consulting in your field.

7. **Write your book and start speaking for a fee.** Travel the world

speaking about your book's topic. Does travel excite you? For some, it excites them to go to new cities or to a country they've never been before.

Well, pack your bags! Writing your book opens the door of opportunity to go places you've never been before. Add speaking about your book's topic to your list of services and watch even more new doors and opportunities for you open.

Are you excited about your increased bottom line waiting for you on the other side of completing your book yet? Don't keep waiting for extra profits to come to you. You could be this time next year looking for that experience. Go ahead; write your book. Then get excited about the profitable things you get to do. Here's to seeing your name in print!

7 INCREASING REASONS
TO WRITE A BOOK

Books are the main source of our knowledge, our reservoir of first faith,
memory, wisdom, morality, poetry, philosophy, history and science.
—Daniel J. Boorstin, Librarian of Congress Emeritus

Have you considered writing a short book to increase your business? Perhaps you are like most of us before taking the leap of faith, you wonder if it will give you the results you dream of. I can tell you this; monetizing your business with a short book will pay you back BIG.

Here are 9 increasing reasons to throw caution to the wind and write your book now:

1. **Increase your self-esteem** by sharing your know-how in your field. People are looking for a friendly expert to show them how to do things faster, easier and with more profit. You know; share all the short cuts & secrets of your business you've learned along the way.

2. **Increase your credibility** as a service expert. When you write a book, you get instant credibility with your colleagues and customers. They are more willing to work with you and trust you faster with book author as one of your titles. Remember, people tend to buy more and do business with people they trust.

3. **Increase your ability to compete.** A book sets you apart from the

non-author colleagues in your field. Write a book this year and receive a boost of profits from your clients because they trust you more than your non-author competitors.

4. **Increase your recognition** by becoming a trusted voice in your field. After writing a book, more people will recognize you. Our societies still look up to authors. It gives you a claim to fame. Write a book filled with how-to, tips, illustrations and checklist. Share your customer success stories through case studies to inspire your audience.

5. **Increase your income** by selling books at your speeches and especially your website. If marketed well, your book can be the beginning of a whole new income stream. After your book is written it becomes your 24 hour sales person promoting your service business everywhere it goes.

6. **Increase your customer list.** One of your most valuable assets in your service business is your customer list. Your book pre-sells your services to each customer that gets a copy. After enjoying your insightful book filled with helpful tips they are more open to purchasing your services.

7. **Increase your list of services.** Write a book and then launch your speaking services, counseling or coaching services with it. Also, you can create other information products as a companion of your book. All designed to further educate and help your service business clients.

8. **Increase your skill base.** Write a book and develop a mini website to sell it on the Internet. If you optimize your book's website well, people will visit it from all over the world and buy it. You may be thinking, I don't know how to build a website much less optimize it. Take a class; hire a computer savvy assistant. If a nontechie person like the author of this book did, you can too.

9. **Increase your ability to help more people.** After writing your book, you gain the ability to reach around the world. Your book

extends the reach of your hands to help others from across town to the other side of the globe. Take advantage of the Internet to promote your book online.

If you don't get started writing your book now, your service business may never receive the increase it deserves. So go ahead; write a book and watch your service business profits explode like a rocket headed to the moon. Here's to seeing your name in print!

CHAPTER 8

7 INSPIRING REASONS TO WRITE A BOOK

Just don't give up trying to do what you really want to do. Where there's love and inspiration, I don't think you can go wrong.

—*Ella Fitzgerald, Jazz Singer*

Are you looking for someone to inspire you? Why not activate the law of reciprocity by inspiring someone else first. Write the book you've been dreaming of writing and you may inspire a whole generation.

You could take your natural wisdom or professional expertise and write it into a book. Your audience is waiting for you to inspire them. They'll love you for it.

They'll buy your book and become fans of yours. They will tell all their friends about your wonderful book. It will happen all because you decided to share your wisdom in a book.

Here are 7 more inspiring reasons to write a book:

1. **Write a book and leave a legacy.** We all leave legacies in our lives to our children or those we have influenced along the way. After realizing that, our job becomes to leave the best legacy we can.

   Aim to fill your book with timeless information. Use principles and laws that aren't subject to change with each season. Write your book this way and it is sure to inspire those in the next generation and beyond.

2. **Write a book and change destinies.** It's intriguing how a couple

of words can make a difference in one's life. Don't be careless with what you put in your book. You have the opportunity to change a heart or mind with your words.

Perhaps you are writing a book to inspire others about your favorite cause. Weigh your words carefully to influence your audience and perhaps change their destiny.

3. **Write a book and inspire others for good.** Inspire others with success experiences that motivate your audience to do more, give more or share more? Share your experiences to motivate your audience.

   Share how you overcame seemingly insurmountable challenges in your life or professional field. It will motivate your audience to think if you did it; they can do it too.

4. **Write a book and activate the law of reciprocity.** The law of reciprocity simply put says what you give out will come back to you. So if you are looking for inspiration, why not give inspiration in your book? It will surely come back to you; usually it comes back in a way you least expect it.

5. **Write a book and create your own destiny.** Take destiny in your own hands and shape your life and future. Stop waiting around for some big name publisher to commission you to write the next best seller. Make your own commitment to write your book and inspire your world in the process.

6. **Write a book and dream bigger dreams.** Many aspiring authors kill their dreams with small thinking. They listen to those around them telling them they can't because neither of you know anyone that did. Be the first; dream a bigger dream. My vote says you can. All you need is one other vote to get it done. That vote is yours. Vote yes; write your inspirational book and inspire those you influence.

7. **Write a book and touch lives.** Will your book offer a fresh perspective of life? Have you been gifted with uncommon wisdom about life in general? Put small excerpts of your understanding

throughout your book. Sprinkle your quotes along with other famous philosophers or world thinkers within your book. For example, if you have special understanding of human nature, bless the global community with it in your book.

Are you excited about inspiring others with your completed book yet? Don't keep waiting for inspiration to come to you. You could be this time next year looking for that experience.

Go ahead; write your very own book and inspire others. Then get in expectancy for the law of reciprocity to work; some wonderful things are coming your way. Here's to seeing your inspirational words in print!

CHAPTER 9

7 MIND BLOWING REASONS TO WRITE A BOOK

You will never be the person you can be if pressure, tension and discipline are taken out of your life.

—*James G. Bilkey, Author*

Do you feel like a stick in the mud when it comes to writing your book? You've come to a stand still, a road block where you can go no further. No worries; you may just need to open your mind a little; change your thinking.

Look for a paradigm shift or a fresh perspective. Before you know it you will be sailing past that impasse blocking your way a few moments ago. At least that's what happened for the author.

Years ago, I was thinking all day about how to get my message out in a bigger way. During the day, I thought briefly about writing a book. I discarded it thinking I didn't have the smarts to do that.

Later in the evening, a friend walked up and said, "What are you waiting on? I know this guy who has written his book and started on another by now. I know you are just as smart as or smarter than he is."

That fresh perspective from my friend was all the push I needed to make it happen. I purchased books, enrolled in courses, asked my friends, made a commitment, wrote my first book and never looked back. Here are 7 mind blowing reasons to help clear your mind and write your book this year:

1. **Write a book and express what YOU have to say.** Don't be a

copycat. Even if you're saying the same thing, find your unique presentation point. Why do you think new fitness books released every year continue to sell well?

It's because every physical fitness trainer, dietician or nutritionist has their unique plan, their unique steps and victorious customers that swear by it.

2. **Write a book and find a commonality with your reader.** You have something in common with every potential reader of your market. For instance, you just wrote a book for new tennis players. Find out what all new tennis players have in common and speak to that commonality in your book.

   It may be that most new tennis players make a certain mistake when serving. Solve that problem for your readers and they will love you. It will create a connection, a sense of knowing. They will feel that you are talking directly to them.

3. **Write a book and increase your communication skills.** Continue to develop your communication skills. As you keep an open mind to learning and improvement, you will become a better educator in your book. Have you wondered why some books are compelling and others are boring?

   Don't get me wrong, I know there are some naturally great communicators. But for most of us, we have developed and perfected our communication skills to become compelling.

4. **Write a book and gain valuable new skills.** If this is your first book, you may have to learn new things to get it done. You may have to take a writing class, a computer class, hire an editor or a book coach. You may have to learn to speak in front of people to promote your book.

   Or you may need to improve your existing skills. Just remember whatever new skills you gain will translate to other areas in your life. New skills will boost your value in the business world and even socially.

5. **Write a book and open the world to your message.** Get rid of

local thinking when it comes to your book. Think global; the world is waiting for your unique message.

After you write your book and it is made available throughout the world, it will be normal for you to receive email and notes from readers in other countries.

6. **Write a book and elevate your consciousness.** Raising your consciousness is the process of seeking, especially through writing a book, to increase awareness of one's role, attitudes, needs, etc. in connection with the personal, social problems of modern life.

   As your message begins to crystallize during the writing process, your book will raise your consciousness of how the solutions inside fit into and make our world a better place.

7. **Write a book and receive a paradigm shift.** Completing your book will open you to a new way of thinking. It may even give you a paradigm shift. Don't do the same things you've been doing for years and expect new results. That's insanity.

   Think outside the box to deliver unique solutions to your reader. Find a system to get your book done fast. Say goodbye to all your friends who say you can't. At least say goodbye until you finish your book. Then re-unite and celebrate your achievement.

So what are you waiting for? Your competitors have already discovered how to put their message into book form. Remember; if you're stuck consider the mind blowing reasons above.

Get a fresh perspective that will carry you to the finish line of a completed book. I can't wait to see your name in print! Best wishes for your book writing project.

CHAPTER 10

6 THINGS YOU ATTRACT MORE OF WHEN YOU WRITE A BOOK

Everybody is like a magnet. You attract to yourself reflections of that which you are. If you're friendly, then everybody else seems to be friendly too."

—*Dr. David Hawkins, Physician and Lecturer*

Are you starting your book project on a shoe-string budget? No worries; many successful authors started the same way. After all, I've been tweeting Charles Schwab's words for months, "The best place to succeed is where you are with what you have." Or recently, the words of Gerald Ford moved me to action, "Begin to act boldly. The moment one definitely commits oneself, heaven moves in his behalf."

So if you're ready to start with what you have and expect the rest to come to you, here's what to do. Decide if you want to write your book now. If so, write your commitment down, align your thoughts, and expect the needed resources to come to you. Even expect the people to show up to guide you. Meanwhile, here are seven right attraction reasons to write a book:

1. **Builds up your magnetism.** When you write your book, you become more magnetic. Author is still a prestigious title. So people will naturally be attracted you as author. They want to be around you and rub shoulders with an author.

2. **Attracts more business.** More people will be attracted to do

business with you. They get to know you through your book and trust you easier. Because you did a good job with your book, they believe you will do a good job for them in business.

3. **Attracts nicer customers.** You can attract nicer customers because of your book. Your message was crystallized to fit. It hits the mark with your book readers. So when it's time to buy a book about your topic, the right people are interested and attracted to you. They want to be nice for they understand you because of your book.

4. **Attracts like-minded people to you.** Your completed book will attract people that think like you. After reading your book, they feel like they know you. They can relate to you and your message; they realize there's little difference between you and them. They feel like if you did it, they can too.

5. **Attracts better opportunities.** Your book will open doors of opportunities. These are doors that may not open unless you have book author as your title. Your book makes you the expert. People love to hear from the expert.

6. **Attracts better offers.** Your book will elevate your prestige, your fame and your credibility. You can expect to receive better offers. For instance, 2 business men are invited to speak at a local business men's luncheon.

   Typically, the business man with the book can expect to receive 4 times as much as the business man without a book. In fact, according to the group's budget they may ask the businessman without a book to donate his services in trade for the exposure.

Don't wait any longer. Start attracting all the good stuff coming your way after writing your book. Make a commitment to write your book this year; heaven is waiting to move on your behalf.

CHAPTER 11

9 EXTRAORDINARY REASONS TO WRITE A BOOK

I believe in taking a positive attitude toward the world. My hope still is to leave the world a little bit better than when I got here.

—*Jim Henson, Muppets Creator*

❧

*H*ave you been thinking of writing a book this year? A New York Times survey accounted that 81% of people feel that they have a book inside them and should write it. According to Toni Morrison, "If there's a book you really want to read, but it hasn't been written yet, then you must write it." Don't let your dream of writing a book fade away. Write your message in a book and release it to the world while it's still in your heart.

Writing a book is still a great way to position you become famous, increase your fees, create added income streams and take more time to be with your family.

A book will elevate your life, add credibility and increase your travel opportunities. Still not convinced? Here are 9 more extraordinary reasons to write your book:

1   **A book creates an enhanced professional image.** After writing your book, you will gain an instant professional image. You will be perceived as a professional person.

2   **A book expands your referral source.** Your completed book becomes your new referral source. More people will want to do business with you as an author. Your book readers will more

readily refer you as well.

3   **A book makes it easier to up sell to your customers.** After reading your book, your customers are easier to up sell to other products. They get to know you and trust you faster for any other products, including higher priced ones.

4   **A book gets media attention.** Your book can open the door to getting the media's attention. You will have to have other things in place to seal it. But with a book, you are more apt to gain the attention and respect from media personnel.

5   **A book builds your name and brand.** You become famous with a book. Of course, you will grow your fame as you promote your book effectively. Your book travels so quickly from place to place. It will grow your name much faster than most any other product.

6   **A book gives you the ability to live anywhere.** As book author, you can live anywhere and work. You don't have to settle in one place for life, unless you want. Many successful authors live in one place for the summer and another for the winter.

7   **A book raises your status.** The title book author is still a prestigious title. So, after you have completed your book your status is immediately elevated. You are respected among the community as a local author. As your name grows, your status will grow beyond your community even unto the world.

8   **A book makes you important.** You will receive special treatment as an author. In all the end of the world movies, they select important and special people to save and start society over again. They choose artist, teachers, authors and musicians, etc. Your book will make you an important person in society.

9   **A book gives you the spotlight.** Your fifteen minutes of fame will come sooner with a book in your list of achievements. You never know when someone has heard of you because of your book and the spotlight swings over to you. Be ready; stay prepared to offer your thoughts.

A close friend complained not long ago about always being put on the spot to speak. She said her husband gently reminded her you are an author and speaker now; you may as well get over it and stay prepared.

Are you ready to join the ranks of successful authors? You don't have to let your message slip away. I can't think of a more opportune way to change your status, grow your brand, and even change your life than by writing a book. Go ahead; write your best book now and prosper.

CHAPTER 12

7 You-nique Reasons to Write a Book

Today you are you. That is truer than true.
There is no one alive that's youer than you!

—*Dr. Seuss*

Have you started your unique book manuscript yet? Write a book and express what YOU have to say. Don't be a copycat; use your perspective. Even, if you're covering the same topic, find your unique presentation point.

Why do you think new weight-loss books released every year continue to sell well? It's because every physical fitness trainer, dietician, weight-loss expert or nutritionist has their unique plan, their exclusive steps and victorious customers that swear by it.

There's still time to get started. For once it's all about YOU. Most of us are too modest. It's about time you did something for YOU and just because YOU want to do it. On that note, here are some You-nique reasons to get started writing your book.

1. You become famous. Many aspiring authors think either you have fame or you don't. They erroneously think the rich and famous are born that way. The truth is most people grow in fame over time. Yes of course there are some that receive fame at birth. So back to (you); when you write your book you become famous. If you write a book and promote it well enough, your fame may just grow to celebrity status.

2. You become an expert. Write a book and become the sought after authority. Become the person everyone refers to in your field. As an authority in your field, people quote you or send all their friends to get information. Continue to grow and learn in your field and put it all in your book. Pull potential book readers in from the entire globe with free articles, reports, white papers and tips to help them.

People are always looking for good information; remember a whopping 85% of Internet users are looking for information. Supply them with good information and they will think of you (a trusted authority in your field) when they're ready to buy.

3. You gain recognition. Increase your recognition by becoming a trusted voice in your field. After writing a book, more people will recognize you. Our societies still look up to authors. It gives you YOUR claim to fame. Write a book filled with how-to, tips, illustrations and checklist. Share your customer success stories through case studies to inspire your audience.

4. You gain respect from your colleagues. Think about it; no one can be you. Even with the same training, the same credentials, a similar skill set you still have a unique perspective. Are you dissatisfied with the way your colleagues treat you?

A client of mine said, "My work associates didn't take my opinions serious until my book came out. Now, I'm constantly asked what I think about the problems that come up."

5. You elevate your lifestyle. Travel the world with your message. Does travel excite you? For some, it excites them to go to new cities or to a country they've never been before. Well, pack your bags!

Writing your book opens the door of opportunity to go places you've never been before. Add speaking about your book's topic to your list of services and watch even more new doors and opportunities for you open.

6. You boost your self-esteem. Believe it or not, there are people waiting to read your book. They already look to you as a leader. Now they are waiting for you to put it in book form. So, don't delay any longer, increase your self-esteem by sharing your expertise in a book.

Most people are looking for a friendly professional to show them how to do things faster, easier and with more profit. You know; share all the shortcuts and secrets of your business you've learned along the way.

7. You increase your skill base. Write a book and hire a web master or develop a one to two page website all about you and your book. Sell it to the world on the Internet. If you learn the basics of SEO (Search Engine Optimization) and optimize your book's website well, people will visit it from all over the world and buy it. Then if they like it, they will tell all their friends about it.

You may be thinking, I don't know how to build a website much less optimize it. Take a class; hire a computer savvy assistant. If a non techie person like the author of this book did, you can too.

Don't procrastinate any more. Make a commitment to write YOUR book this year; your audience is waiting to get to know you. Make it different, make it count and make it YOURS. I'm looking forward to seeing your name in print!

CHAPTER 13

21 SIGNIFICANT REASONS TO WRITE A BOOK TO SELL

You must see your goals clearly and specifically before you can set out for them. Hold them in your mind until they become second nature.
—*Les Brown, Speaker*

⁂

Are you ready to test your book's significance? Have you asked the tough question, "Will my book sell?" Everyone wants to know before they invest time, effort and most of all money. If your book proves significant then it is salable.

Here are a few tips to help you know if your book will sell well before you even write it. Give your manuscript the test of significance. Write your book to meet two to three areas to achieve significance and most of all sales in the book marketplace.

1. **Write a book to help your readers gain a new skill?** Thousands of people search for specific information daily. They want simple to read and easy to understand information. Seek to educate your audience; include engagement tools in your book. They may want to learn how to change their car oil or build a deck. Educate your audience and your book becomes significant.

2. **Write a book to solve the problems for your targeted audience?** Get this right and you could have a best seller. Do you know how to solve the top problem for your audience? Write the solution and the steps in your book. You might be surprised at who's searching

for a little relief from a pressing problem. Remember, problems come in all sizes, shapes and categories. Solve one problem and add more as you write. Then fit as many solutions as you can into your book without making your information overwhelming.

3. **Write a book to offer expert advice, inspiration, hope to a specific group of people?** Target a group of people within your broad market. Your target group could be single dads, moms or working moms. For example, the Chicken Soup series for Teen-Agers, Mothers, even Prisoners sold much better that the original more general Chicken Soup for the Soul.

4. **Write a book and offer opportunities to learn interesting facts?** Sprinkle your book with little known interesting trivia about your topic. Be careful to avoid filling your book with detailed statistics and diagrams.

    But do sprinkle facts and trivia as morsels throughout your book. Doing so will create anticipation that leads your readers through to the end. You'll find, people love statistics and bite-sized trivia about just about any topic.

5. **Write a book with an easy to read style?** Take a complex subject in your field and make it simple. Most people enjoy an easy reading language. The Dummies series catapulted this concept to new heights with all kinds of complex subjects made simple.

    Your readers will not only reward you by reading to the end but they will be happy to tell all their friends about your insightful easy to read book.

6. **Write to book to offer new, different information?** Have you wondered what makes a revised and expanded book sell well even when there are similar books on the market?

    The author promises new, different or added information. People can't resist the bait of new and different. Even if it's the original book the author offers a new and different perspective than competing books already on the market.

7. **Write a book to inspire people to do something good?** Intertwine

inspirational stories into your book and sell more. For example, the *21 Irrefutable Laws of Leadership* spent 18 straight months on the *Business Week* Business Best Seller List. Dr. Maxwell started each chapter with a short story of a famous person successfully using the chapter's law of leadership. At the time of this writing, Elizabeth Gilbert's *Eat, Pray, Love* book spent a long season on the best selling lists and then was made into a movie because of her inspiring story (memoirs).

8. **Write a book to entertain and make people laugh.** Do you have an ability to make people laugh? Use it in your book. Create a little haven of escape for your readers. People love it when you entertain them. In fact, it's one of two basic reasons people read anything.

   You can even interweave funny stories into your non-fiction manuscript. Seek to entertain your audience, make them laugh; they'll love you for it.

9. **Write a book to offer wisdom about life?** Have you been gifted with a deep understanding about life? Yes, then put small excerpts of your wisdom throughout your book.

10. Use your quotes along with other famous philosophers or world thinkers inside your book. For example, if you have a special understanding of human nature, spiritual wisdom and understanding, bless the worldwide community with it in your book. **Write a book to offer a greater understanding of nature?** Are you passionate about nature and its beauty? Perhaps you want to make strides in preserving our planet Earth. Write about it in your new book and share it with the world.

   Who knows you may move a whole generation. The Baby Boomer generation is talking about Jacques Cousteau books, inventions and documentary films of the ocean.

11. **Write a book to present great perception of animals?** For instance, if you have a deep understanding of animals the animal lovers will lap your book information up. (smile)

    Write a book and fill it with your special understanding of

animals. Express your passion well and you could be next Horse Whisperer Monty Roberts or Dog Whisperer Celan Milan.

12. **Write a book to offer success experiences that motivate your audience to do more, give more or share more?** Share your experiences to motivate your audience. Share how you overcame seemingly insurmountable challenges in your life or professional field. It will motivate your audience to think if you did it; they can do it too.

13. **Write a book to help people save money.** They may want to invest for the future or save for a big purchase. They want to free up cash in their budget during the recession. Or they may just be looking for a bargain. Write a book that helps others save lots of money and you may have a top seller on your hands.

14. **Write a book to offer ways to save time.** Most people want to work less and spend time enjoying their family and life's pleasures. Even if you just put time-saver tips in your book, it will be more appealing to a broader audience.

15. **Write a book to help others look better.** Perhaps your audience wants to lose weight, tone their body, or improve their facial features. Your content is significant if it makes them feel more attractive.

16. **Write a book to help people live longer.** A new wave of people groups want to get in shape, eat better or gain extra energy. Help people live longer; your book will be significant and make them feel healthier.

17. **Write a book to help others feel loved and desired**. Many don't want to be lonely anymore or want to start dating again. Show them how to re-enter the dating game. Or you could simply show them how to be single and happy. Write a book that makes them feel wanted.

18. **Write a book to help others in their marriage**. There are lots of couples who don't have a clue as to how to gain a successful marriage. Do you have a special compassion for struggling couples?

Write your book filled with marriage success tips and encouraging words for a marriage on the rocks.

19. **Write a book to help parents raise a family**. There are no manuals passed out before parents start a family. If you have special insight to help parents raise toddlers, teen-agers or anything in between, fill your new book with this information. Do it right and you could have a top seller on your hands in no time.

20. **Write a book to help people gain friends** and be popular. They may want to be a famous celebrity or be more popular in school or work. Your book will make them feel praised and admired.

21. **Write a book to assist your audience in gaining pleasure.** They may want to satisfy their appetite or sexual desires. This will make them feel more fulfilled.

According to experts of the ten significant areas, your book need only have:

1 for a newspaper or magazine article

2 for a significant book

3 for a best seller

5 for a Pulitzer Prize

6 for literary classic

Are you ready to start writing yet? Did your book idea pass the test of significance in at least two areas? Great, it will sell! Now that you know your book is significant, go ahead take the plunge. Don't hesitate any longer. Your audience is waiting for your unique ideas and viewpoint. Make it different. Make it count. Make it yours.

CHAPTER 14

7 WAYS TO MAKE YOUR BOOK OUTSELL ITS COMPETITION

Do your little bit of good where you are; its those little bits of good put together that overwhelm the world.

—*Desmond Tutu, Activist and Christina Cleric*

*H*ave you wondered if your book could stand out in the marketplace and sell? The way to make your book stand out in a crowded market is to target a niche market related to your book's topic. Identifying a niche is really hot in the marketing world right now and rightly so. You may remember these principles from an earlier lesson. Some principles are worth repeating. Even so, I'll make sure to keep the repeating to a minimum.

Simply put, to target a niche market in your book's topic area: Identify a problem/solution and research your competition. Then develop a different approach. With all the books in the world on your topic, it's not enough to know the solution. You must present the solution in a different way than existing books do.

Develop a way of making your book different. You need a different viewpoint, a niche, or a different spin on perhaps the same information. Examine the problem again. Look at the solution your book solves with the goal of coming up with a way to present your knowledge differently than existing books.

Here are seven simple ways to do this:

1. **Market Segment.** You can develop a niche by focusing on an occupation, sex, or age group, i.e. Lose 14 Pounds in 2 Weeks: A Guide for Women Above 40, Lose Weight Safely Before, During & After Pregnancy.

2. **Broadening Market.** Consider appealing to a broader market: Lose 14 Pounds in 14 Days: A Guide for Working Class Men & Women.

3. **Focus.** Attack a big problem by emphasizing a particular tool or technique that you have experience with. For example, show how heart attack survivors can lose 14 pounds in 2 weeks by eating only fish, white meats and walking 10 miles a day.

4. **Program.** I love this one. Base your solution on the way you solve a large problem by breaking it into steps, i.e. Write Your Best Book Now: An 7 Step Program for book writing.

5. **Expertise.** Base your niche on your market's previous experience with a topic, i.e. The Last Business Book You'll Ever Need!

6. **Goal.** Organize your existing information around benefits of achieving the goal: Free Again, Healthy Again!

7. **Affinity.** Perhaps you have a relationship with a high visibility organization that has benefited from your ideas; you can reframe your knowledge by leveraging off your association: The Bank of America Financial Program or the Southern Methodist University Weight Loss Program.

You may have noticed in each one of the above examples of the same market, the contents of the book would probably be the same! The books would contain the same basic ideas, suggestions, tips, etc. For example, all the books about diets would probably stress the importance of eating right, choosing the right foods in right portions and daily exercise. Yet, each book presents a different viewpoint targeting a different market.

So BE BOLD; have no fear about approaching the same subject as existing books. Focus in on your unique ideas and viewpoint. Remember, according to the writer of Ecclesiastes, "There's nothing new under the sun." Bernice Fitz–Gibbon said so eloquently, "Creativity often consists of merely turning up what is already there. Did you know that right and left shoes were only thought up only little more than a century ago." Now go start your successful book journey. Make it different. Make it count. Make it yours.

CHAPTER 15

21 WRITING MISTAKES THAT MAY STAMP S.T.A.L.E. ON YOUR BOOK

Hold yourself responsible for a higher standard
than anybody else expects of you.

—Henry Ward Beecher

Have you eaten stale crackers, recently? Not long ago, I rushed into a little neighborhood grocery store to grab a few things. One of the items I grabbed was a box of crackers. I rushed home, prepared dinner, pulled out the box of crackers and bit into one. It was stale! You know; it tasted like paper, dry, no crisp. The salt had even lost its saltiness.

Speaking of stale, are you making the mistakes that stamp S.T.A.L.E. on your book? If you're anything like the writer, when she first began writing books, you could be making some simple mistakes that will hinder the success of your book.

No worries; now you don't have to make those same mistakes, you can put a stop to the little mistakes that make your book writing S.T.A.L.E. in a big way. Here are 21 mistakes and how to avoid them. Put them into action and receive trailer truck loads more book sales and triple times the success you were expecting. All because you wrote a compelling book and refused to write copy stale as crackers.

So, are you ready to draw readers to your book like metal to a magnet? No worries; then you must do some things differently. You can't keep doing things the same and expect different results. That's insanity.

All it takes is a different perspective. Change your perspective; your important message and book will draw all the readers it deserves. Here are 21 writing mistakes to correct that will draw readers like a magnet to your book.

1. Failure to know your message is significant. Write with confidence and authority. Put away your fears and doubts once and for all. With all the great books written, there's only one voice that's uniquely yours. I am convinced there are people waiting for your perspective, your solution, or your message. They're waiting to be inspired, entertained or helped by YOUR book.

2. Failure to write for your readers. Don't be self serving. Discover what your readers want. Then write a book filled with what they want to read. They will love you for it and read everything you write. To top it off, your book will make you famous and sell beyond your wildest dreams. All because you put aside what you wanted and gave your audience what they wanted to read.

3. Failure to make it simple. Use simple language. Avoid technical jargon that may confuse your readers. Aim for seventh and eighth grade level communication. Write your book in an active voice. Cut the passive voice and create compelling copy.

4. Failure to create readable copy. Don't bog your readers down with schoolbook terms and stuffy language. Choose words like caution instead of admonish or get instead of garner. Become a friendly mentor offering advice and results oriented tips inside your book and more people will be drawn to you and your writing.

5. Fail to use stories. Tell stories in your book. Stories will help you connect with your readers on an emotional level. Many readers may not remember much of what you are teaching. Tell a story with your material; they will remember you and your stories.

6. Fail to give application. More than anything, your readers want you to tell them how to do it in simple language. Whether you are explaining how to bath the baby or wash the puppy, people want you to give them step-by-step guidelines. Fill your book with application and you will win more readers.

7. Failure to put your reader first. Most of us write selfishly. I mean we write what we want. Go against the natural grain; give your readers what they want. Write to their benefit. Write a solution to their problems.

8. Failure to begin well. Create a sizzling beginning. Hook your readers through emotion. Slant your book or introduction with a question or an amazing statistic. Share the top benefits of your book early. Aim for the 'You' in every reader.

9. Failure to break your writing into short sections. Write your book in chunks, chapters, sections and parts. Use headings, bulleted lists, pull quotes and other easy reading tools. Don't make your chapters too long. Create easy transitions to the next chapter or section. Keep each section short and easy to read.

10. Failure to use short sentences. Slash your sentences to under 15-17 words. Don't bog your readers with complex sentences. Remember multiple phrases slow your reader's comprehension. Make it easy. Get to the point fast.

11. Failure to use simple words. Write for the 7-10 grade level. The shortest, most well-known words are best. The more syllables in a word, the less compelling it becomes. Cut all unnecessary adjectives. Clear, easy to understand copy makes your reader want to read your piece to the end. Fill your writing with what's in it for them. They'll come back for more and tell all their friends.

12. Failure to avoid technical jargon. Unless you are writing a technical manual where most everyone will understand the technical language, don't use technical jargon. It will become techno mumbo jumbo to your readers; they will find something better to do besides figure out what you're saying.

13. Failure to be specific. Avoid generalities. Engage your reader's emotion with specifics. Let them experience color, size and shape. Instead of,

"Complete your degree online fast to increase your income." Say, "Complete your master degree online fast so you can upgrade your lifestyle, get vacations, health insurance and other corporate benefits." Specific benefits create a stronger pull than the general benefit of increased income.

14. Failure to slash adverbs. Go through and cut words like openly, suddenly, very that tell the reader instead of show the reader. Circle all the (ly) and (very) words. Pull out your thesaurus and replace them with power words that show emotion or describe.

15. Failure to check the flow of information. Check your paragraphs for good harmonic flow and understanding. Meaning, make sure you don't drop off suddenly and change the subject. Clear writing creates compelling copy. Compelling copy leads to more book sales.

16. Failure to slash passive structures. Passive sentences slow and dull your writing. Get rid of the passive voice sentences. Give your sentences a clear subject and a verb to avoid the passive voice. "The writer found fame and fortune through marketing her books online." instead of "The writer's books were instrumental in leading her to fame and fortune." Avoid connecting verbs like 'was', 'is', 'had', and 'seemed'. Replace passive voice verbs with active verbs.

17. Failure to seek to entertain your readers. Use analogies, stories, illustrations and case studies. Even if it's a manual or a simple non-fiction book, put interesting facts and statistics throughout the pages. You can create teaser paragraphs or relief box stories. Relief from what you may ask? Relieve them from the important but boring details. Sprinkle theme stories related to your book's content in a box in each chapter. Boxing the story will give your reader a brief break from the normal reading.

18. Failure to seek to educate your readers. I know it's been said many times that nothing's new under the sun. But do your best to not re-hash old information. Don't be afraid of research. Or at least, visit the research companies that specialize in gathering facts and statistics about certain topics. Pull little known stats and facts for your field or industry.

19. Failure to write your book with soul or passion. Write with all the professionalism you can muster but write from the heart. Write with passion; write with soul. Strategically place your statistics and famous quotes but don't be stuffy with your language. Your readers may think you are talking down to them if you use too many technical terms and professional jargon.

20. Failure to use your teachable moments. There are two main reasons people read. One of those reasons we read is to be educated. Take advantage of the teachable moments from your life. It will make your book more interesting. Remember, the stale cracker moment above. The author tied it in with the staleness our writing can have.

21. Failure to empathize with your reader. Write a book that personally connects with your audience. Do you connect with your reader emotionally? You should express empathy with your reader and their problems.

Empathy is the capability to share and understand another's emotions and feelings. It is often characterized as the ability to "put oneself into another's shoes." Let them know you've walked where they've walked. Or you are in close relationship with someone who has and you understand their feelings and emotions

Are you ready to give your book the magnetic pull that keeps readers reading to the end? Correct the mistakes above and write sizzling copy that your readers find hard to put down?

Remember to put your reader first, develop a sizzling start, break your writing into short sections, shorten sentences, use simple words, avoid technical language and be specific. Implement the strategies and tips above to begin writing a compelling book! Now go; write a successful book and make us all proud!

ACTION STEPS

1. What one reason will motivate you to take action before your head hits the pillow tonight?

_____

_____

_____

2. Which reason will you commit to acting on by the end of the week?

_____

_____

_____

3. What are some obstacles you can predict might get in your way?

_____

_____

_____

4. What is your plan for successfully dealing with these predicted obstacles?

_____

_____

_____

5. When you can put any combination of the reasons to write a book to action, what will you be able to do that you cannot do now?

_____

_____

_____

ABOUT AUTHOR

Earma Brown is a 16 year author, book writing coach and iWIN founder. She received a Bachelor degree in Business at University of Arkansas. She has written 12 books including two other iWIN books from the Write to Win Series, eBook It and Article Marketing Speedway. Earma lives in Dallas, Texas with her husband Varn Brown.

OTHER SIGNATURE RESOURCES BY EARMA BROWN

eBook it!

http://ebookitsuccess.com

Article Marketing Speedway ePackage

http://www.articlespeedway.net

40+ Article Writing Templates ePackage

http://www.40articlewritingtemplates.com

Book Writing Course – 12 week online course

http://www.bookwritingcourse.com

Self Publish Your Book ePackage

http://www.selfpublishyourbooknow.com

100 DAYS COURSE BOOK

12 Week Book Writing Course (online)
http://100daystoabook.com

Uncover the best way to get your wildly successful book written fast! For all the details on a proven program that walks you through 12 amazingly simple lessons to get your BEST book written and out to the world. Now is better than later. Visit us at the *Write to Win Section of Butterfly Press Books for this companion workbook* "Write Your Best Book Now: *How to Write a Book In 100 Days or Less!*"

(Also Now available in paperback)

http://www.butterflypress.net/store/

BOOK ORDER INFORMATION

To order more books:

Butterfly Press/ Earma Brown
P.O. Box 180141
Dallas, Texas 75218

Visit Butterfly Press Books   http://butterflypress.net/store/

RESOURCES

International Writers Information Network
http://www.writersinformationnetwork.com/

Book Writing Help
http://bookwritinghelp.com
http://bookwritingcourse.com
http://writetowin.org

Book Publishing
http://butterflypress.net
http://innercourtpublishing.com

Author Services, Book Cover Design, Book Trailers
http://scriberecreative.com

NOTES

NOTES

NOTES